Courtesy of Tulikivi

Fire Spaces

Design Inspirations for Fireplaces and Stoves

Fire Spaces

Design Inspirations for

Fireplaces and Stoves

Tina Skinner

Schiffer Publishing Ltd

4880 Lower Valley Road, Atglen, PA 19310 USA

Library of Congress Cataloging-in-Publication Data

Skinner, Tina.
Fire spaces: design inspirations for fireplaces and stoves / by Tina
Skinner.
p. cm.
ISBN 0-7643-1694-X (Hardcover)
1. Fireplaces--Design and construction. 2. Stoves--Design and
construction. I. Title.
NA3050 .S58 2002
721'.8--dc21
2002007583

Front cover: Top, *Courtesy of FireSpaces, Inc./Moberg Fireplaces,*
Center, *Courtesy of Tulikivi.* Bottom right, *Courtesy of FireSpaces/
Moberg Fireplaces.*
Back cover: Top left, *Courtesy of Jøtul North America.*Top right,
Courtesy of FireDesigns. Center, *Courtesy of Hy-Lite Products, Inc.*
Bottom left, *Courtesy of FireSpaces, Inc./Moberg Fireplaces.* Bottom
right, *Courtesy of Tulikivi.*
Half title page: *Courtesy of Empire Comfort Systems, Inc.*
Title pages: *Courtesy of DL Ackerman Design Group*

Designed by Bonnie M. Hensley
Cover design by Bruce M. Waters
Type set in Zurich LtXCn BT/Zurich BT

ISBN: 0-7643-1694-X
Printed in China

Published by Schiffer Publishing Ltd.
4880 Lower Valley Road
Atglen, PA 19310
Phone: (610) 593-1777; Fax: (610) 593-2002
E-mail: Schifferbk@aol.com
Please visit our web site catalog at
www.schifferbooks.com

This book may be purchased from the publisher.
Include $3.95 for shipping. Please try your bookstore first.
We are always looking for people to write books on new and related
subjects.
If you have an idea for a book please contact us at the above
address.
You may write for a free catalog.

In Europe, Schiffer books are distributed by
Bushwood Books
6 Marksbury Avenue
Kew Gardens
Surrey TW9 4JF England
Phone: 44 (0) 20-8392-8585; Fax: 44 (0) 20-8392-9876
E-mail: Bushwd@aol.com
Free postage in the UK. Europe: air mail at cost.

Acknowledgements

The seeds for this book were gleaned from the Hearth, Patio, and Barbecue Association's literature and website. That organization provided the safety tips and a glossary of terms. There is no better source for fireplace facts and figures, as well as manufacturer and distributor information. Visit their website at www.hpba.org.

Additionally, I met wonderful people within the fireplace manufacturing industry who helped make this book possible. Plus, many, many thanks to the interior designers whose talents make this the beautiful and inspiring book that it is.

Courtesy of Sroka Design, Inc.

Contents

Courtesy of Laurence Taylor

Introduction

Courtesy of Empire Comfort Systems, Inc.

Fire is a mesmerizing focal point for our lives and our homes. Staring into a safely contained fire soothes us on some primitive level that no doubt harkens back to the dawn of mankind. For many of us, it is a meditation we rarely indulge in: relaxing completely in warmth, staring into glowing embers and dancing flames, and letting our minds go. Our troubles go.

With friends and family, a fire is stimulus for conversation, fuel for jokes and camaraderie. Pauses in conversation aren't awkward, there's a fire to attend to, a focus for fleeting attentions.

Everyone loves to play with fire. To toss twigs on, to shift burning logs, to push back hot embers. Toasting marshmallows is a cherished childhood memory, and a closely supervised parent-child project.

As a child myself, our little-used fireplace was always lit on Christmas morning. In front of its glow, we experienced the magic of Santa-delivered surprises. Without a fireplace, how would Santa get inside, and where would we hang our stockings?

A hearth is an absolute essential, according to homebuilder statistics. Though the average American household lights a fire only three times a year, homebuilders don't dare leave out the fireplace – they can't sell a house without one. Even in sunny states, a fireplace is the key component of almost every living room. A sure way to impress people is to have not one, but two fireplaces, or more. And a home with fireplaces in unconventional places – the bedroom or bath, the kitchen, or the sunroom – is sure to draw rave reviews.

As the images in this book will show, fireplaces adapt easily to any room in the home. The facings, mantels, and surrounds can be dressed up, down, or practically disappear to suit the needs of the homeowner. They're darlings for interior decorators, with a rich assortment of styles ranging from formal marble and carved stone facades, to sleek contemporary fire surrounds, to cozy, charming, country-style cast iron stoves.

What's more, the fire spaces available to today's homeowners are much more versatile, and infinitely safer than those of yesteryear. High-tech innovations allow for fuel efficiency in addition to greatly increased heating capacity for the home (should you want it). Remote controls can be used to create gas fire with the flick of a button; self-feeders allow pellet stoves to burn for up to 24 hours without tending; vent-free technology allows a fire space to be set up in the middle of a room or against an inside wall – the possibilities are almost endless.

Then there's the look! This book is all about the style of fire – the settings we build to house it, using elaborate mantels and spacious hearths, wrought-iron surrounds and shiny brass trim. Here, in hundreds of pictures, we explore how fire spaces can be adapted to formal rooms where we entertain, family spaces where we gather, and intimate spaces where we escape to read a good book, or take a long soak in a hot tub. Today's modern hearth products allow you to create your own style, from a simple stove like those used a century ago, to an elaborate two-story stone mantel resembling something straight out of a palace in Europe. Pick a simple fire pit that will create an instant (gas powered) bonfire on your deck, or build yourself a solid stone fireplace that will radiate heat and warm your household hours after the fire flickers out.

Here is an opportunity for the members of a household to gather in front of their own fire and talk about ways to improve or expand upon their fire spaces. Start with the room where you want a fire, or to improve an existing fireplace, and then ask yourselves a few important questions. Are you creating a new fire space, or replacing an existing fireplace or stove? Is this fireplace for heating the home or simply for aesthetic appearance? How much of the home do you want to heat? Is this a backup system to your furnace during power outages? What level of convenience do you want? What fuels are accessible to you (firewood, natural gas, propane, wood pellets, coal, oil, electricity)?

Fireplaces

A fireplace is the most popular choice for homeowners. Unlike its predecessors built of brick and mortar, today's fireplaces are factory-built fireboxes enclosed within a steel cabinet. These fireboxes are subjected to rigorous testing standards established by Underwriters Laboratories and the American Gas Association and have an excellent safety record. Besides being safe, they are surprisingly affordable. They use a lightweight chimney and do not need any additional footing or structural support. Freed from the restrictions of a site-built masonry fireplace, factory-builts are surprisingly simple and inexpensive to install.

Today's fireplaces are available in a nearly limitless variety of styles, and the possibilities are truly exciting. Fireplaces can be open on one, two, three, and even four sides, allowing 360-degree viewing.

Fireplace Inserts

Fireplace inserts are primarily used to change an existing non-efficient fireplace into an efficient, heat producing zone heater. Inserts can be retrofit into an existing masonry or factory-built fireplace. They offer superior efficiency for burning wood, gas, or wood pellets, and most have blowers to circulate heat.

Stoves

Stoves are very efficient little heaters and are generally used to warm a specific room or zone of the house. They are available in a wide selection of sizes and styles, and are made of steel, stone, or cast iron, with finishes including porcelain enamel and high temperature paint. Space-age ceramic glass can provide fire viewing. Stoves may burn wood, gas, coal, wood pellets, or oil – all resulting in gentle radiant heat the epitomizes cozy on a cold winter day.

Masonry Heaters

When it comes to burning wood, masonry heaters are among the cleanest and most efficient options. Ideal in cold climates, masonry heaters use a stone mass to absorb the heat from small, hot fires. That heat is then radiated as gentle warmth over time. Today's models combine time-tested traditional European designs with state-of-the-art engineering. More expensive and requiring solid foundations, masonry units only have to be fired once or twice a day.

False Fireplaces

False fireplaces are a popular option for someone who doesn't want to go to the expense or trouble of a fire-ready installation. The advantages lie in the fact that a false fireplace creates a beautiful overall look for the room, but is not a permanent fixture. Instead, a lovely mantel, a surround, and a cover might be used to simply create the impression that a fire well lies beyond.

Mantels of Yesterday sells restored mantels as well as antique "summer covers." The company recommends choosing the mantel you want, and then starting with a piece of plywood cut slightly larger than the mantel opening. The plywood is then faced with false brick wallboard, paver brick, ceramic or marble tile. A "Summer Cover" can then be attached, and the entire piece screwed to the back of the mantel opening. When the mantel is placed against the wall, it looks complete.

Fueling Your Fire

Wood is the original flame feeder, and continues as the most popular choice. Few, in fact, are aware of the many attractive alternatives available today.

If a wood fire is what you want, today's fireplaces and stoves offer less pollution and more energy efficiency than ever before. The amount of smoke emitted by woodstoves has been reduced by an average of 90 percent, and almost all wood-burning stoves and inserts sold today are certified by the federal Environmental Protection Agency as clean burning. Less smoke also means less potentially flammable creosote in the chimney system, making it safer than ever to enjoy a fire in your home. Wood is a renewable resource, and is available in most areas.

There are lots of alternatives to a stack of wood outside your home, though. Pellets are a clean-burning, renewable resource made from compressed sawdust. Poured into a hopper, they can be automatically fed to a stove and burn for up to 24 hours.

Coal is a clean burning fuel source, producing no visible smoke or creosote. Further, coal stoves can burn longer per fuel load than woodstoves and provide even, controllable heat.

Oil and natural gas are also options for reliable room heating, and an electric fireplace can simulate a gentle wood fire without a chimney or venting system, and can even be programmed to provide the right amount of warmth.

Tips for Safety and Efficiency

Clear the area around the fireplace and chimney. Debris too close to the fireplace could cause a fire. Check the flue for obstructions like birds' nests, and trim any overhanging branches or large trees near the chimney.

Always use a fireplace screen.

Never overload the fireplace with too many logs. Don't use the fireplace as an incinerator, and never burn garbage, Christmas trees, or piles of paper.

Keep a fire extinguisher on hand and place smoke detectors throughout the house. Test the smoke detectors and batteries regularly. See that the extinguisher is in good working order and that all family members know how to operate it.

When building a fire, place logs at the rear of the fireplace, preferably on a grate.

Never leave fire unattended. Be sure the fire is extinguished before you go to bed.

Keep wood stacked, covered, and out-of-doors, away from the house and off the ground. Bring in only as much as you need for one evening to prevent insects that may be in the wood from entering your home

Have your fireplace inspected annually and cleaned when necessary by a chimney sweep certified by the Chimney Safety Institute of America. A dirty fireplace can cause chimney fires and inhibit proper venting of smoke up the flue. It can also contribute to air pollution. Your local NCSG-certified chimney sweep will diagnose your fireplace and recommend what it needs in order to burn cleanly and safely.

Choose the right fuel. In general, hardwood firewood (oak, madrone, hickory, ash, etc.) burns cleaner than softwood firewood (fir, pine, cedar, etc.).

Use seasoned wood, wood with a moisture content of less than 20 percent, burns much cleaner than green (high moisture content) wood. Check with your cordwood supplier to make sure that the wood you purchase is seasoned.

Burn smartly. Good fireplace habits can decrease fuel consumption in the home while maintaining the same level of warmth. Make sure the fire gets enough air to burn properly. Close the damper when the fire is out to keep warm room air inside.

Make a fire that fits your fireplace. A fire that's too large or too hot not only wastes fuel, it can crack your chimney.

Keep your fireplace in good working condition. If you notice any cracks in the chimney, and any loose mortar or brick, have your chimney repaired. Have the chimney liner inspected for cracking or deterioration.

Read and follow the label when using manufactured fire logs. Use one fire log at a time, starting it with a fireplace at room temperature. Don't poke or break manufactured logs. This will cause them to crack apart, releasing their energy at a high rate and resulting in a shorter burn time. Fire logs perform best when burned on a supporting fireplace grate with a maximum of three to four inches of space between support bars.

If your fireplace is equipped with glass doors, leave them open while burning a fire log to allow proper draught and cleaner burning. Once you're sure the fire is extinguished, close the damper and glass doors to retain warm air inside the house.

THE GOLDEN GATE BRIDGE · DEDICATED MAY 27, 1937

Family Rooms

Everyone piles in here, to watch TV, play games, or simply to relax in each other's company. The family room is where we come together, away from our chores – homework, housework, food preparation, and daily hygiene. This is where we simply are together and at our happiest.

Opposite page: Almost like installing a built-in cabinet, this gas fireplace was installed on an inside wall. *Courtesy of Empire Comfort Systems, Inc.*

A calming meadow-green color on the walls dispelled the harshness of a cathedral ceiling, and softened the edges of a wonderful, fieldstone fireplace. *Courtesy of The Glidden Company*

A seaside view frames a classic brick and pine surround and a modern gas fire. *Courtesy of Montigo DelRay*

This room is rich in Arts and Crafts style, from the furnishings to the one-of-a-kind brick and tile surround and the cross-sectional wood that rise above it. *Courtesy of Travis Industries, Inc.*

Dark upholsteries and wood finish create a warm retreat where one can get lost in the glow of the fire. *Courtesy of Travis Industries, Inc.*

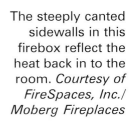

The steeply canted sidewalls in this firebox reflect the heat back in to the room. *Courtesy of FireSpaces, Inc./ Moberg Fireplaces*

A stone chimney rises two stories through an exposed post-and-beam home. A hand-hammered wrought iron face forms a neat frame for the wood fire. *Courtesy of Travis Industries, Inc.*

Rocks and gold create an unforgettable corner in this cozy family room. *Courtesy of Travis Industries, Inc.*

Direct-vent technology allowed these homeowners to squeeze a fireplace into this half wall, flanked by a hi-fi sound system. *Courtesy of Travis Industries, Inc.*

An arched cutout holds fire, display shelves, and sunlit leaded glass windows – a beautiful, show-off wall. *Courtesy of Travis Industries, Inc.*

A pretty blue pellet stove becomes a centerpiece in a classic country sitting room. *Courtesy of Nu-Tec Incorporated*

A warm gas fire draws household members to comfy chairs and a collection of favorite books. *Courtesy of Mendota*

Simplicity of design in a tile fireplace surround allows for great flexibility in designing a room. Above the fireplace, a painting creates the illusion of a small, bay window. *Courtesy of Sroka Design, Inc.*

A gas stove introduces heat in a cozy, old-fashioned style to a traditional post-and-beam room. *Courtesy of Napoleon Fireplaces*

Golden walls reflect the glow of fire and sunlight. *Courtesy of Travis Industries, Inc.*

Black and white furnishings fit with black fireplace surround and blonde woodwork. *Courtesy of Travis Industries, Inc.*

A fireplace is sandwiched in fieldstone and topped by white crown molding and a copper vent. *Courtesy of Travis Industries, Inc.*

A crisp neat room reflects a feminine touch. Here friends and family are invited to warm their bones with hot tea and flames, and good-spirited competition. *Courtesy of Travis Industries, Inc.*

Stone is a no-brainer in a log cabin, and the rest of the furnishings were equally well chosen for this heavy timber room. *Courtesy of Travis Industries, Inc.*

Cultured Stone® rises to the top of a cathedral ceiling, becoming the centerpiece in an impressive great room. *Courtesy of Cultured Stone® Corporation*

Manufactured stone veneer has been cast and colored to exactly imitate alluvial stone in this artful corner fireplace display. *Courtesy of Cultured Stone® Corporation*

A hand-carved relief panel in the mantel creates a centerline between falling water above and roaring fire below. *Courtesy of Travis Industries, Inc.*

Opposite page, top: A gas stove works with hand-woven rugs, exposed beams, stucco, and ceramic tile to create a wonderful, Southwestern atmosphere. *Courtesy of Harman Stove Co.*

Opposite page, bottom: Tile and a red oak mantel surround this fireplace and reflect the warm tones that typify this room. *Courtesy of Grand Mantel, Inc.*

Top center: Glowing embers and six lit logs belie the gas-fueled nature of this cozy fire. *Courtesy of Montigo DelRay*

A tall, brick fireplace surrounded by tile reaches skyward, while a lengthy mantel creates a low-water level in a high-ceilinged room – achieving an arresting centerpiece. *Courtesy of Sroka Design, Inc.*

Black tile extends from a simple fireplace frame to a lengthy hearth perfect for displaying art, and for fireside seating. *Courtesy of Toby Zack Designs, Inc.*

© Dan Forer

A colorful painted mantle carries the carpet's colors. *Courtesy of Sroka Design, Inc.*

Asian influence is reflected in recurring elements – black squares, an antique chest of drawers, and a raised fire platform. *Courtesy of Vermont Castings*

Animal prints, sleek black marble and dark wood finishes create a modern, exotic aura lit by fire. *Courtesy of Harman Built Fireplaces*

Layers of cut and polished marble create a contemporary look in this fireplace surround. *Courtesy of Travis Industries, Inc.*

A see-through fireplace offers a glimpse into another room, tantalizingly obscured by two walls of acrylic block. *Courtesy of Hy-Lite Products, Inc.*

Although it blocks a little window, this gas stove adds a lot of view, creating warmth on a bright autumn day. *Courtesy of Harman Stove Co.*

A gas stove inserted in an alcove adds fire without cleanup concerns. *Courtesy of Harman Stove Co.*

A woodstove becomes a piece of furniture, radiating warmth and adding an excuse to cover a wall in earthy red brick. *Courtesy of Vermont Castings*

Opposite page: A vent-free gas fireplace can be installed against any wall of a home. *Courtesy of Empire Comfort Systems, Inc.*

Black-finish on a steel facing creates the look of cast iron for this gas fireplace frame, a wonderful addition to a room full of classic furnishings. *Courtesy of Montigo DelRay*

Windows high above an extended, wall-long mantel create the feeling that one is in a sunken retreat, warmed by fire and cushioned by carpet and soft upholstery. *Courtesy of Travis Industries, Inc.*

Direct-vent technology allows for a garden view over the mantel in this cozy space, where the width of the room is intimate, but the cut-out ceiling soars. *Courtesy of Travis Industries, Inc.*

An oak cabinet works in a room of natural tones.
Courtesy of Empire Comfort Systems, Inc.

Brick and wood were painted to match, creating a seamless effect of broad mantel and built-in cabinetry, with a gas insert at its heart. *Courtesy of Travis Industries, Inc.*

Wonderful architectural details – a fireplace carved from stone, exposed timbers in a cathedral ceiling, and built-in cabinetry – give this room an aura of old world or country French style. *Courtesy of Design Specifications and Nasrallah Fine Architectural Design*

A wonderful, circular hearth forms a stage for a cast-iron woodstove. *Courtesy of Nu-Tec Incorporated*

Cast concrete imitates cut stone in this simple yet elegant fireplace surround. *Courtesy of DESA™ International*

39

Bob Narod Photography

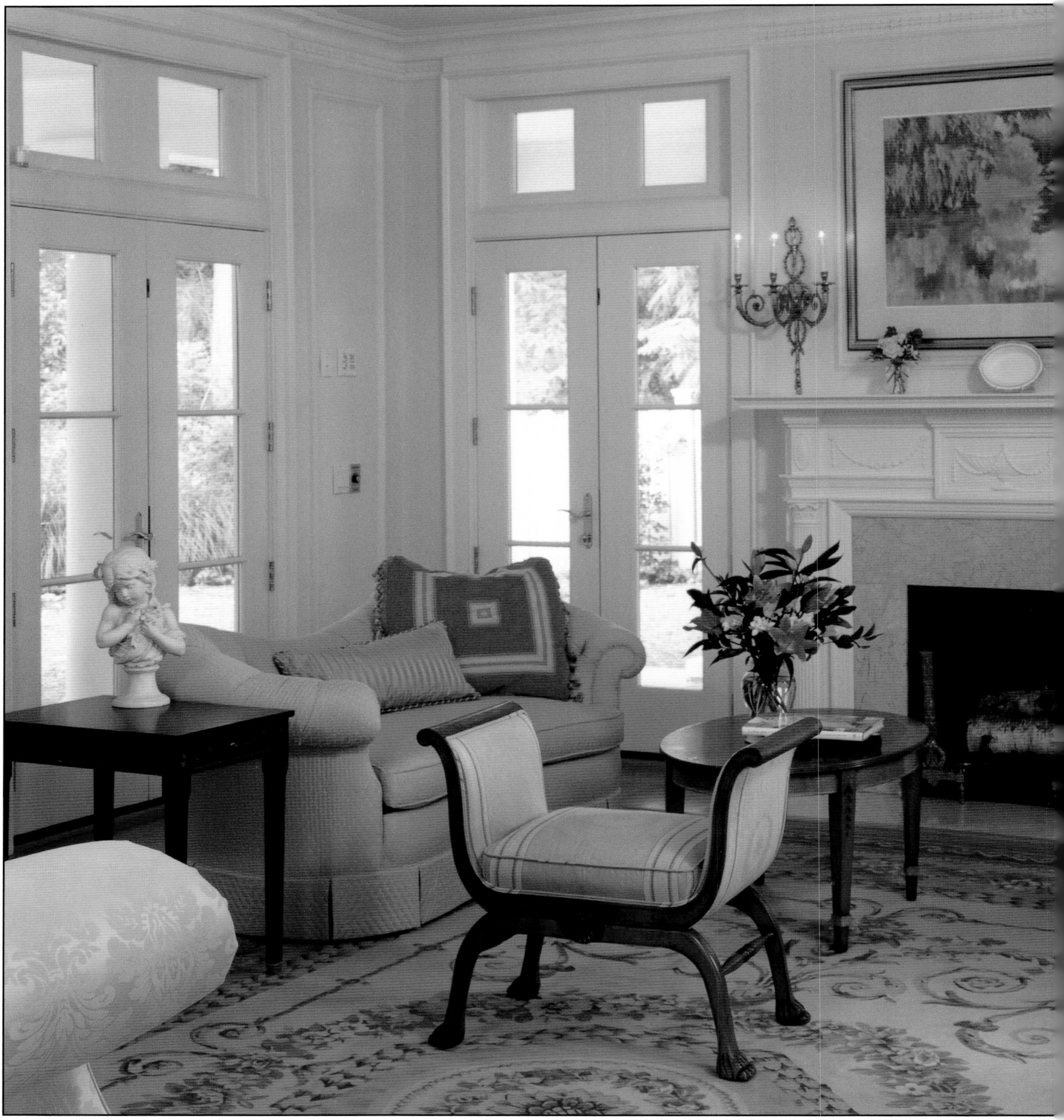

Living Rooms

Often a little used room, these are our home's showpieces – where we put our best furniture, our best pictures and art. So it is not surprising that few living rooms lack a fireplace. It is almost a mandatory appointment for the symbol of our proud home ownership.

Classic design elements in woodwork and textiles create a formal air for this lovely, light-filled sitting room. *Courtesy of Sroka Design, Inc.*

A fireplace can vent straight through the wall,
allowing for sunlight above, firelight below.
Courtesy of Hy-Lite Products, Inc.

Opposite page: Fancy woodwork in Louis XV style fills this room floor to ceiling. At the heart of this amazing assembly of hand-carved wood sits the fireplace. *Courtesy of Architectural Paneling, Inc.*

An impressive mantel rises amidst built-in cabinetry to fill a grand, two-story living room. Brass magnifies the fire's warmth. *Courtesy of Mendota*

Custom cabinetry, columns, and a classic mantel create the illusion of an 18th Century parlor. Yet they surround an eye-fooling modern gas fire – no logs are hauled across this spiffy white carpet. *Courtesy of Travis Industries, Inc.*

Feminine flair is evident in the accessories of a smart little sitting room, rich in architectural moldings. *Courtesy of Travis Industries, Inc.*

Symmetry in the architecture branches out from a fireplace, framed from the hallway by columns. *Courtesy of Travis Industries, Inc.*

A fireplace becomes an excuse for art in faux marble and tile. A mirrored backdrop lights the interior of the fireplace, doubling its appearance as a showplace. This two-sided fireplace shares the firebox with the sunroom. *Courtesy of Sroka Design, Inc.*

An elaborate mantel and surround work with a lush collection of antiques in this formal sitting room. Antique cast flower pots make a wonderful summer stand-in for logs and andirons. *Courtesy of Sroka Design, Inc.*

46

A pellet stove adds reliable, easy-to-maintain warmth to a formal sitting room, fitting neatly within the original Marble surround. *Courtesy of Travis Industries, Inc.*

Whites work with metallic hues for neo-classic elegance. *Courtesy of Travis Industries, Inc.*

Taupe tones surround
a fireplace, where a
nickel-plated face and
veined marble create
a contemporary feel.
*Courtesy of Travis
Industries, Inc.*

Creamy colors allow
the important things to
stand out – the art, the
fresh flowers, and the
fire. *Courtesy of Travis
Industries, Inc.*

Cherubs romp above
a fire, where a
modern insert has
been fitted into a
classic old fireplace.
*Courtesy of Travis
Industries, Inc.*

A tapered Cultured Stone®
fireplace surround supports a lofty
mantel amidst custom cabinetry.
*Courtesy of Cultured Stone®
Corporation*

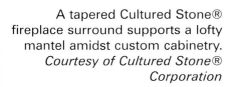

49

A fireplace and wet bar share double billing in an elaborate, Louis XV-style paneled room, finished in antique white. *Courtesy of Architectural Paneling, Inc.*

A brick ledge becomes a popular perch when the fire is lit and folks are drawn into the living room by its warmth. *Courtesy of Travis Industries, Inc.*

Fluted columns extend above the mantel to create a natural frame for art and other above-fire displays. *Courtesy of Travis Industries, Inc.*

A beautiful steel surround and black mantel treatment gives this room elegant flare. *Courtesy of Harman Built Fireplaces*

Stonework soars toward a high ceiling in this classic fireplace surround. *Courtesy of Travis Industries, Inc.*

Massive candles pay homage to the larger fire. *Courtesy of Travis Industries, Inc.*

52

A white surround contains the fireplace in this decidedly feminine sitting room. *Courtesy of Majestic Fireplaces*

Traditional elegance in surrounding woodwork and traditional furnishings create a classic aura for this new home. *Courtesy of Sroka Design, Inc.*

53

A wrought-iron screen mirrors the arch of a curved limestone surround. Beyond, a masonry firebox has been canted toward the center to efficiently reflect heat into the room. *Courtesy of FireSpaces, Inc./Moberg Fireplaces*

Candles and a mirror are traditional toppers for the living room fireplace. *Courtesy of Majestic Fireplaces*

A bay-front insert creates a tidy fire in a fieldstone chimney. *Courtesy of Travis Industries, Inc.*

A wall of manufactured precast stone and a fireplace are the focus of a six-sided room, where a wide-screen television plays right-hand man. *Courtesy of Cultured Stone® Corporation*

Wood and precast stonework create zones in a wall that zigs and zags for visual interest. *Courtesy of Cultured Stone® Corporation*

A manufactured stone veneer wall mimics fieldstone from Napa Valley in this wonderful, custom fireplace surround. *Courtesy of Cultured Stone® Corporation*

A half-round of log punctuates a dramatic rise of stone above the fireplace. *Courtesy of Cultured Stone® Corporation*

58

Black marble in mantel and hearth create defining lines in a wall of stonework and fire. *Courtesy of FireSpaces, Inc./Moberg Fireplaces*

Chunky timbers and slate tiles were pooled for classic arts and crafts style in this living room. *Courtesy of Travis Industries, Inc.*

Two quarries were mined to create this beautiful surround an ultra-clean burning masonry fireplace, set in a wondrous wall of windows. *Courtesy of FireSpaces, Inc./Moberg Fireplaces*

Warm tones in faux bois wood and leather surround a emperador brown marble fireplace. *Courtesy of Sroka Design, Inc.*

A golden glow is created floor to ceiling in this fire-warmed room. *Courtesy of Travis Industries, Inc.*

A unique exhibit of molding and artwork crowns this handsome fireplace. *Courtesy of Travis Industries, Inc.*

63

A catalytic gas fireplace shares the view with a wall of windows. *Courtesy of Lennox Hearth Products*

Set amidst a pretty arrangement of arched windows, a beautiful, bay-front fireplace warms the winter scene beyond. *Courtesy of Mendota*

A fireplace competes for attention with the lake beyond, a fact accounted for in the positioning of furnishings. *Courtesy of Travis Industries, Inc.*

Stylish woodwork creates an appealing frame for a long, narrow, fireplace. *Courtesy of Lennox Hearth Products*

Gothic girl painting adds glamour and mystery to a stunning room done in black and white. Below, a fire can be lit to add glow to the girl and her admirers. *Courtesy of Toby Zack Designs, Inc.*

Art Deco effect in the tile surround works with the waterfront view to add blue to a room of whites and creams. *Courtesy of Travis Industries, Inc.*

A green-tiled fireplace is the focus of a contemporary sitting room. *Courtesy of Travis Industries, Inc.*

Color is happily incorporated into a penthouse suite, warmed by a pellet stove that was capped with an honorary mantel plank. *Courtesy of Travis Industries, Inc.*

Fire sheds warmth on an entryway, under the half wall of a colorful living room. *Courtesy of Travis Industries, Inc.*

A metallic finish on mantel and fireplace create memorable affect. *Courtesy of Majestic Fireplaces*

Great Rooms

The popular "great rooms" that are at the heart of today's newest homes. In these rooms the family's primary gathering areas are adjoined into one – kitchen, dining, and family/living room. A nook may even be devoted to a home office or entertainment system. One thing that's never left out, however, is the fireplace.

A great room – sitting, dining, and cooking areas rolled into one – wouldn't be complete without a fireplace. Here a direct vent fireplace insert enjoys the starring role. *Courtesy of Empire Comfort Systems, Inc.*

A soaring stone mantel climbs the chimney in this two-story room, creating a classic focal point amidst Mediterranean architecture. *Courtesy of Design Specifications and Ross Design Group*

Circular seating focuses all eyes on an amazing curved wall of manufactured stone veneer. *Courtesy of Cultured Stone® Corporation*

Chris Wren Construction/Michael Lowry Photo

Manufactured stone cast and colored to imitate ledgestone and fieldstone rises in tiers up this two-story outside wall, creating a dramatic presentation and housing a flat-screen television and fire. *Courtesy of Cultured Stone® Corporation*

An arched doorway frames an impressive, two-story exposed chimney of concrete cultured to look like fieldstone. *Courtesy of Cultured Stone® Corporation*

Eric Figge Photography, Inc.

Brass facing helps a fireplace compete for attention with a stone chimney that soars into great wooden rafters. *Courtesy of Harman Built Fireplaces*

Cultured Stone® mimics white river rock, working beautifully with whitewashed logs. *Courtesy of Cultured Stone® Corporation*

An artful wooden mantel frames equally artful stone-work in cast and colored concrete on this two-story fireplace. *Courtesy of Cultured Stone® Corporation*

A display of foliage on the mantel adds to the earthy appeal of Cultured Stone® surrounding the fireplace. *Courtesy of Cultured Stone® Corporation*

Iron, wood, and precast stonework soar above fire in this contemporary post-and-beam home. *Courtesy of Cultured Stone® Corporation*

78

Warm Nooks

At the other end of the room-scale spectrum, it's always nice to curl up in a small warm place, alone with a book or favorite album, or together with a favorite companion. A crackling fire and an intimate space draw us back to a sense of security as ancient as our cave-dwelling ancestors.

The ultimate in self indulgences: a comfy chair, a warm fire, and a reading lamp. *Courtesy of Tulikivi*

A pellet stove sends heat up a stairwell, and warms a cozy reading nook. *Courtesy of Travis Industries, Inc.*

A gold-planted fireplace sits flush on a short tile wall. *Courtesy of Travis Industries, Inc.*

Spare lines create a minimalist approach in this decorator's scheme, allowing artworks to stand out. Among them, the custom marble mantel makes a bold Art Deco statement, underlined by a basket packed with ripe wheat stalks. *Courtesy of Sroka Design, Inc.*

Arts and crafts paneling and chairs frame a stone fireplace. *Courtesy of Travis Industries, Inc.*

Grandmother and grand-child have appropriately sized rockers, where they can sit and compare wisdom of the ages. *Courtesy of Travis Industries, Inc.*

A matching pair of wicker chairs are perched by fire and view. *Courtesy of Travis Industries, Inc.*

A corner model gas fireplace illuminates a comfy sitting area. *Courtesy of Lennox Hearth Products*

Tile, stucco, and glass block create a modern wall, at the center a warm gas fire. *Courtesy of Lennox Hearth Products*

A neutral palette was chosen for its ability to create calm in this dining room. A corner fireplace is simply adorned, a quiet place that comes to life when a fire is lit. *Courtesy of The Glidden Company*

Built-in seats frame fire and view. *Courtesy of Lennox Hearth Products*

This versatile gas freestanding stove can be installed anywhere, even venting through the floor. *Courtesy of Central Fireplace*

This direct-vent freestanding stove has a millivolt ignition system, meaning it can operate without electricity in the event of a power outage. *Courtesy of Central Fireplace*

His and hers chairs flank a fireplace. *Courtesy of Travis Industries, Inc.*

A modest investment in space, this small gas unit adds enormous warmth and romance to a breakfast nook. *Courtesy of Vermont Castings*

A charming mix of handcrafted country accents define this intimate fireplace setting. *Courtesy of Travis Industries, Inc.*

Warmth greets the weary outdoorsman upon entry. *Courtesy of Travis Industries, Inc.*

A mix of greens and floral reds create year-round holiday cheer, complete with a cozy fire. *Courtesy of Travis Industries, Inc.*

Textiles and brick add to the exotic blend of earthen colors around a brick fireplace with modern insert. *Courtesy of Travis Industries, Inc.*

A brass bucket sits ready to reload a pellet stove, in a room where the owner goes to warm up and relax. *Courtesy of Harman Stove Company*

A coal fire warms a room rich in wood and stone. *Courtesy of Harman Stove Co.*

The gas fireplace has evolved into a clean, safe, convenient way to provide a warm, comfortable environment in the home. *Courtesy of Montigo DelRay*

A red finish on a pellet stove offers a bold style statement, in an apartment where the owner embraced color. *Courtesy of Harman Stove Co.*

A corner fireplace allows these homeowners to create a cozy gathering place in a small family room. *Courtesy of Grand Mantel, Inc.*

91

Kitchen and Dining Rooms

When guests come we all hang out in the kitchen. Once you manage to move them to a table for dinner, it's likely that no one will leave that spot. So why not have the fire where the friends and family will be?

Only recently has fire begun moving back into the kitchen, where it was once a necessity for food preparation. Chefs and hobbyists are rediscovering fire's contribution to cuisine, and fireplaces that double as pizza and bread ovens are soaring in popularity.

A fireplace is an historic fixture in a kitchen, here with a backwoods twist in a rustic, second home. Here a stone-encased wood oven makes the perfect pizza or foccia. *Courtesy of Plain & Fancy Custom Cabinetry*

94

A contemporary mountain chalet is warmed in winter by a masonry heating unit – a solid soapstone fireplace where wood heat is absorbed and then evenly radiated into the room. *Courtesy of Tulikivi*

The warmth of a wood fire is absorbed by solid soapstone in this corner fireplace unit, which will radiate heat evenly for hours, even after the fire goes out. *Courtesy of Tulikivi*

A wonderful idea – a gas fireplace sits at eyelevel with diners, ready to cast a warm glow at a moment's notice. *Courtesy of Cultured Stone® Corporation*

Lighted alcoves by a Cultured Stone® surround create a warm nook in a dining area. *Courtesy of Cultured Stone® Corporation*

A see-through fireplace warms diners on either side of the divide. In the kitchen, it is housed in a wonderful wall of custom cabinetry built to house the owner's eclectic collectibles. *Courtesy of Kitchen Company*

A peninsula fireplace unit allows views of the fire from three sides in this open kitchen and family area. The tile surround changes from one side to the other, graduating from black and white to a more subtle, yet colorful surround in the sitting area. *Courtesy of Design Specifications*

A stove stands sentinel between eat-in kitchen and a family room. *Courtesy of Travis Industries, Inc.*

A pellet stove provides warmth, and doesn't block a bit of the wintry view. *Courtesy of Travis Industries, Inc.*

103

A metallic blue finish on a woodstove works with the blue theme in this family dining/seating area. *Courtesy of Empire Comfort Systems, Inc.*

A peninsula gas unit allows the creation of an island that brings a surround sight fiery view. *Courtesy of Napoleon Fireplaces*

Pine finish on a mantel surround for this electric fireplace contributes to a cheerful, country atmosphere. *Courtesy of Vermont Castings*

A see-through unit fits neatly under a countertop, creating heat for two rooms, working space above. *Courtesy of DESA™ International*

An entire living area benefits from an efficient gas fireplace that produces 22,000-32,000 Btu/hour. *Courtesy of Lennox Hearth Products*

A see-through gas fireplace offers a clean face to both diners and relaxers in separate rooms. *Courtesy of Lennox Hearth Products*

A see-through fireplace sheds warmth on both living room and dining room. *Courtesy of Majestic Fireplaces*

Photography by David F. Noyes Studios

A peninsula unit brings the look and warmth of a wood-burning fire to two rooms, and can be viewed from three sides. *Courtesy of DESA™ International*

Gold trim adds formality around this fireplace, a focal point in a formal living room. *Courtesy of Majestic Fireplaces*

107

A gas fireplace adds sunshine to a beautiful backyard view. *Courtesy of Majestic Fireplaces*

A peninsula unit radiates heat in three directions, offering more than 1,800-square-inches of viewing area within a home. *Courtesy of Lennox Hearth Products*

Black accents add contemporary flare to a dining area. *Courtesy of Vermont Castings*

Stylish furnishings get an added aura of glamour in the glow of a peninsula fireplace. *Courtesy of Montigo DelRay*

Library & Den

A classic male domain, these rooms are creeping back into today's new homes. A booming economy and an emphasis on entertaining and working at home have made the traditionally dark, paneled rooms all the rage. Here are some classic examples that wouldn't be the same without the inclusion of a blazing fire.

Custom paneling defines the room's centerpiece – a gorgeous fire crackling in a brass and marble surround. *Courtesy of Empire Comfort Systems, Inc.*

112

In the manner of 18th Century craftsmanship, this gas fireplace commands a central role in hand-crafted wood paneling, complete with hand-carved moldings, all stained a rich tone. A collection of Chinese antiques reflects the owner's travels. *Courtesy of Sroka Design, Inc.*

A classic library, where the men retire after dinner for a drink. *Courtesy of Travis Industries, Inc.*

Built-in cabinetry houses the homeowner's favorite books, and invites one to linger nearby as the temperatures drop outside. *Courtesy of Travis Industries, Inc.*

An English style mantel and bookcases frame the fire in this handsome library. *Courtesy of Architectural Paneling, Inc.*

113

Eighteenth century style is recaptured with a slate surround and a hand-carved, painted mantel. *Courtesy of Architectural Paneling, Inc.*

Crowned by an English-style mantel and over mantel, this fireplace is framed by open top walnut bookcases. *Courtesy of Architectural Paneling, Inc.*

Manufactured precast concrete stone appears as river rock in a wonderful fireplace surround, complete with an arched cutout for firewood, and a great ledge for sitting next to the fire. *Courtesy of Cultured Stone® Corporation*

Bronze horses prance across a mantel, poised over a rock and brick chimney and flanked by built-in cabinetry. *Courtesy of Travis Industries, Inc.*

A desk and an easy chair flank a classic fireplace. *Courtesy of Travis Industries, Inc.*

A free-standing gas stove can be quickly fired up to warm a home office. *Courtesy of Montigo DelRay*

A contemporary setting was created for this easy on and off gas fireplace. *Courtesy of Mendota*

A collection of African art is arrayed around a see-through fireplace surrounded by brass and black marble. *Courtesy of Monessen Hearth Systems*

A central fireplace allows viewing from two sides, radiant heat all around for this open floor plan. *Courtesy of Tulikivi*

Baked to a rock-hard finish, these porcelain stone tiles work with a carved stone mantel to create a fireplace and floor that will outlast generations. *Courtesy of Crossville Porcelain Stone/USA Company*

A fascinating contrast is created between marble grays of porcelain tiles and a rich hunter green on the walls. Dark wood finish in the shelving, and a black finish on the corner stove complete the relaxed atmosphere. *Courtesy of Crossville Porcelain Stone/USA Company*

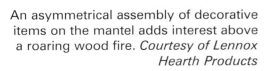

An asymmetrical assembly of decorative items on the mantel adds interest above a roaring wood fire. *Courtesy of Lennox Hearth Products*

Bed and Bath Rooms

Fire, flame, and heat define romance, so what could be more romantic than a fireplace in the bedroom? Of course, hauling wood and tending to a fire could easily douse a romantic moment. Once upon a time, a fireplace in the bedroom was the only way to keep it warm. Otherwise, homeowners were forced to carry hot coals from a fire elsewhere to warm a frigid bed before climbing in. In a world where furnaces take care of cold winter nights, cleanliness and ease-of-use are more important issues, especially in rooms associated with relaxation. So the advent of remote-controlled, instant fire has ushered in the popularity of bedroom fireplaces. An even greater luxury is a fire-lit bath, and today's new homes often include master baths spacious enough to accommodate both the claw-foot tub and a fireplace.

Rose and blue punctuate a dramatic white room. Light is a standout element in crystal chandelier, a silver mirror, and a wonderful white fireplace surround. *Courtesy of Sroka Design, Inc.*

Fire reflects perhaps most naturally within a green and gold atmosphere. *Courtesy of Majestic Fireplaces*

White defines a feminine boudoir, where an electric fireplace was installed (no construction necessary) to cast a warm glow. *Courtesy of Vermont Castings*

The heat vents to a guest room are often closed during the winter. An electric fireplace creates a quick fix for a cold occasional room. *Courtesy of Vermont Castings*

River-polished stones provide a backdrop for a gas-fired stove, warming a cozy bedroom. *Courtesy of Travis Industries, Inc.*

Arches extend from the top of a fireplace to above the window – adding architectural accent to this beautiful bedroom. *Courtesy of Harman Built Fireplaces*

Painting the mantel to match the walls adds to the dreamlike atmosphere of this romantic room. *Courtesy of Majestic Fireplaces*

129

A bedroom becomes both quiet library retreat and romantic getaway, warmly lit by fire. *Courtesy of Crossville Porcelain Stone/USA Company*

A peninsula-shaped gas fireplace is part of a warm ledge where one can disrobe for a relaxing soak. *Courtesy of Montigo DelRay*

An intimate setting, this fire-lit space offers an opportunity to soak in a view while washing away worries and cares. *Courtesy of Sroka Design, Inc.*

A see-through gas fireplace combines two romantic fantasies – a glowing bedside fire, or a long soak by firelight. *Courtesy of Napoleon Fireplaces*

Vent-free technology allows the installation of a fireplace on an inside wall, adding instant romance to this bedroom. *Courtesy of Empire Comfort Systems, Inc.*

A cast-iron stove warms a loft bedroom. *Courtesy of Jøtul North America*

A corner whirlpool can be lit by daylight, filtered through acrylic block, or by night with an easily ignited gas fireplace. *Courtesy of Hy-Lite Products, Inc.*

A gas fireplace lies ready to softly light a magnificent little bath nook, awaiting only the warm water, salts, and soaps. *Courtesy of Design Specifications*

Gallery of Great Hot Spots

Here are more than 100 great fireplaces to study close-up, including flush-face fireboxes and bay-fronts, hand-carved wood mantels and exquisite tile surrounds, stone and stucco, brick and big pot bellied stoves. Enjoy!

Courtesy of Montigo DelRay

Courtesy of Montigo DelRay

Courtesy of Montigo DelRay

Courtesy of Majestic Fireplaces

Courtesy of Montigo DelRay

Courtesy of Montigo DelRay

Courtesy of Lennox Hearth Products

Courtesy of Lennox Hearth Products

Courtesy of Lennox Hearth Products

Courtesy of Lennox Hearth Products

Courtesy of Lennox Hearth Products

Courtesy of Majestic Fireplaces   *Courtesy of Lennox Hearth Products*   *Courtesy of Montigo DelRay*

Courtesy of Lennox Hearth Products

Courtesy of Montigo DelRay

Courtesy of Mendota

Courtesy of Lennox Hearth Products

Courtesy of Napoleon Fireplaces

Courtesy of Lennox Hearth Products

Courtesy of Lennox Hearth Products

Courtesy of Napoleon Fireplaces

Courtesy of Design Specialties

Courtesy of Lennox Hearth Products

Courtesy of Cultured Stone® Corporation

Courtesy of Lennox Hearth Products

Courtesy of Mendenhall Wood Carving

Courtesy of Mantels of Yesteryear

Courtesy of Mantels of Yesteryear

Courtesy of Montigo DelRay

Courtesy of Mantels of Yesteryear

Courtesy of Mantels of Yesteryear

Courtesy of Mantels of Yesteryear

Courtesy of Mantels of Yesteryear

Courtesy of Napoleon Fireplaces

Courtesy of Central Fireplace

Courtesy of Mantels of Yesteryear

Courtesy of Cultured Stone® Corporation

Courtesy of Cultured Stone® Corporation

Courtesy of Napoleon Fireplaces

Courtesy of Central Fireplace

Courtesy of Tulikivi

Courtesy of Lennox Hearth Products

Courtesy of Lennox Hearth Products

Courtesy of Napoleon Fireplaces

Courtesy of Travis Industries, Inc.

Courtesy of Superior Fireplace by Lennox

Courtesy of Cultured Stone® Corporation

144

Courtesy of Cultured Stone® Corporation   *Courtesy of Cultured Stone® Corporation*   *Courtesy of Cultured Stone® Corporation*

Courtesy of The Glidden Company

Courtesy of Jøtul North America

Courtesy of Travis Industries, Inc.

Courtesy of Grand Mantel, Inc. and Travis Industries, Inc.

Courtesy of Lennox Hearth Products

Courtesy of Travis Industries, Inc.

Courtesy of Travis Industries, Inc.

Courtesy of Lennox Hearth Products

Courtesy of Travis Industries, Inc.

Courtesy of Lennox Hearth Products

Courtesy of Travis Industries, Inc.

Courtesy of Travis Industries, Inc.

Courtesy of Grand Mantel, Inc. and Travis Industries, Inc.

Courtesy of Grand Mantel, Inc.

Courtesy of Travis Industries, Inc.

Courtesy of Mendota

Courtesy of Lennox Hearth Products

Courtesy of Napoleon Fireplaces

Courtesy of Thermo-Rite Mfg.

Courtesy of Lennox Hearth Products

Courtesy of Central Fireplace

Courtesy of Lennox Hearth Products

Courtesy of Napoleon Fireplaces

Courtesy of Lennox Hearth Products

Courtesy of Lennox Hearth Products

Courtesy of Hearth Classics, Travis Industries, and Grand Mantel

Courtesy of Napoleon Fireplaces

Photography by David F. Noyes Studios
Courtesy of DESA™ International

Photography by David F. Noyes Studios
Courtesy of DESA™ International

Photography by David F. Noyes Studios
Courtesy of DESA™ International

Photography by David F. Noyes Studios
Courtesy of DESA™ International

Courtesy of Sroka Design, Inc.

Courtesy of Majestic Fireplaces

Courtesy of Crossville Porcelain Stone/USA Company

Courtesy of Crossville Porcelain Stone/USA Company

Photography by David F. Noyes Studios
Courtesy of DESA™ International

Courtesy of Travis Industries, Inc.

Courtesy of Lennox Hearth Products

149

Courtesy of Napoleon Fireplaces

Courtesy of Napoleon Fireplaces

Courtesy of Lennox Hearth Products

Courtesy of Central Fireplace

Courtesy of Lennox Hearth Products

Courtesy of Lennox Hearth Products

Courtesy of Lennox Hearth Products

Courtesy of Lennox Hearth Products

151

Courtesy of Jøtul North America

Courtesy of Jøtul North America

Courtesy of Travis Industries, Inc.

Courtesy of Travis Industries, Inc.

Courtesy of Travis Industries, Inc.

Courtesy of Lennox Hearth Products

Courtesy of Lennox Hearth Products

Courtesy of Travis Industries, Inc.

Courtesy of Travis Industries, Inc.

Courtesy of Lennox Hearth Products

Courtesy of Vermont Castings

Courtesy of Vermont Castings

Courtesy of Lennox Hearth Products

Courtesy of Lennox Hearth Products

Courtesy of Lennox Hearth Products

Courtesy of Travis Industries, Inc.

Courtesy of Travis Industries, Inc.

Courtesy of Lennox Hearth Products

Courtesy of Lennox Hearth Products

Courtesy of Napoleon Fireplaces

Sunrooms and Beyond

A three-season rooms becomes four when you stick in a fireplace or stove. Expanding upon the theme, fireplaces and stoves are moving out of doors, luring us out on cool autumn evenings to sit around a fire, or welcoming spring and burning away cabin fever. Outdoor fireplaces and cooking centers are one of the hottest trends in residential landscaping today. The pictures explain why.

A gas stove warms a bright sunroom, making this addition to a home a year-round attraction. *Courtesy of Empire Comfort Systems, Inc.*

A garden room is warmed in winter by a roaring gas stove. *Courtesy of Travis Industries, Inc.*

A lofty apartment takes advantage of the view with huge sheets of glass – a corner stove compensates for the heat loss. *Courtesy of Travis Industries, Inc.*

A corner stove surrounded by windows radiates heat into the home's most popular room. *Courtesy of Travis Industries, Inc.*

A gas stove adds fire to a watery view. *Courtesy of Travis Industries, Inc.*

A pedestal stove keeps a sunroom addition warm. *Courtesy of Vermont Castings*

A three-sided peninsula unit warms a sunroom where artwork indoors overlooks nature's art outside. *Courtesy of Monessen Hearth Systems*

Interior and exterior are tied together by Cultured Stone® in the courtyard walls and an exposed chimney. An outdoor fireplace casts light on a small pond, and a fire inside offers views from three directions. *Courtesy of Cultured Stone® Corporation*

A wall of Cultured Stone® creates a privacy barrier and a safe spot for a warm fire on this open porch. *Courtesy of Cultured Stone® Corporation*

An outside wall of this home got a makeover in concrete that was cast and tinted to replicate real stone. A built-in barbecue and fire pit provide the glow. *Courtesy of Cultured Stone® Corporation*

A fireplace defines the perimeter of a patio, and beckons people to gather there. *Courtesy of Majestic Fireplaces*

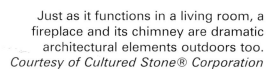

Just as it functions in a living room, a fireplace and its chimney are dramatic architectural elements outdoors too. *Courtesy of Cultured Stone® Corporation*

163

Eric Figge Photography, Inc.

A roaring fire beckons one out to the edge of a grand patio, defined by columns and topped by beams and pure sky. *Courtesy of DL Ackerman Design Group*

Opposite page: A cast-aluminum chimenea was adorned with a raised leaf pattern to create a hot topic for conversation. It is gas operated for ease of use. *Courtesy of Empire Comfort Systems, Inc.*

A two-way fireplace sheds light under an overhang and out toward a balcony, with wide hearth ledges on either side for seating on crisp evenings. *Courtesy of Cultured Stone® Corporation*

Dramatic design – an arched fireplace surround, a stonewall, and a stucco chimney — was created using various decorative concrete casting techniques. *Courtesy of Cultured Stone® Corporation*

The FirePit is an inexpensive way to bring a wood fire onto the deck or patio, tailgating, camping, or onto the beach. *Courtesy of Whalen Manufacturing Company*

This Asian-inspired aluminum
and stainless steel
Luminarium™ fires up with the
turn of a switch. *Courtesy of
Fire Designs*

A classic fire pit, a ring of stones, but this one contains ceramic logs lit by gas. *Courtesy of Vermont Castings*

This gas patio fireplace in a stately cast-iron base is a handy, portable unit that takes fire to gathering places undefined by ceilings. *Courtesy of Vermont Castings*

Glossary

BTUs - British Thermal Unit, the primary heat measurement unit used by the hearth industry. It is the amount of heat required to raise the temperature of one pound of water by one degree Fahrenheit.

Catalytic Combustor - a device used on some wood burning stoves to reduce the temperature at which smoke is ignited.

Clearance - the distance required by building and fire codes between stove, smoke pipe or chimney and combustible materials such as wood materials, furniture, or carpets. Clearances must be obeyed even if noncombustible plaster or other masonry materials protect the combustible materials.

Creosote - a very flammable byproduct of combustion that can build up within the smoke pipe and chimney and then ignite, causing "chimney-fire."

Direct Vent Appliance - an appliance that draws combustion air from outdoors and exhausts all combustion products to the outdoors, eliminating the need for a standard chimney system. A glass panel in direct vent units is critical to keeping the combustion system sealed from the home, maintaining high efficiency and indoor air quality.

Emissions - byproducts of combustion vented out of the home.

EPA Regulations - government regulations of wood burning appliances mandating that products sold after July 1, 1992, emit no more than 4.1 grams of particulate matter per hour for catalytic-equipped units and no more than 7.5 grams for non-catalytic-equipped units.

Firebacks - protect fireplace masonry and mortar, shielding them from extreme heat of the flames. Cast-iron firebacks store heat from the fire and radiate it into the room after the fire has died down. Firebacks work just as well in a modern gas fireplace as they do in a traditional wood burning one.

Fireplace Inserts - heating units that retrofit into an existing fireplace (masonry or factory-built). They burn wood, gas, or wood pellets and offer superior efficiency.

Flue - vent or chimney for a combustion device.

Freestanding stove - a heating appliance normally on legs or a pedestal that occupies an area roughly equal to that of an easy chair.

Gas Logs - provide dramatic realism from the lifelike ceramic fiber, concrete, or refractory logs down to the glowing embers. Manufactured log sets have a burner that uses either natural gas or propane.

Glass Doors - close off the opening of the hearth so heat from the central heating system does not escape up the chimney when the fireplace is not being used.

Grate - an iron frame used to hold burning fuel in a fireplace.

Hearth - traditionally refers to the floor of a fireplace on which a blaze is built. Today it is also used to refer to all the devices and equipment used in connection with the fireplace and the stove industry.

Heat Shield - a noncombustible protector used around appliances, smoke pipe, or chimney.

Hopper - a container attached to an appliance in which fuel, either coal, nuggets, or wood pellets, is stored and from which the fuel is fed to the burner.

Island Fireplace - a fireplace that has four sides of glass, for viewing from any angle.

Mantle or Mantel - an ornamental facing surrounding the fireplace or simply a shelf above a fireplace.

Metal Liner - used primarily with fireplace inserts and placed inside an existing chimney (usually masonry) to reduce the diameter of the flue for more rapid exit of smoke and combustion gases. Also used when an existing chimney is unlimited or deteriorating.

Natural draft (B-vent) Appliances - a gas-burning appliance that takes in combustion air from the home and vents products of combustion outside the home.

Pellets - made of 100 percent wood sawdust with no additives. The sawdust in pellets is a manufacturing byproduct otherwise destined for landfills.

Peninsula Fireplace - a fireplace that has three sides of glass.

Steamers - kettle-like steamers, available in a wide range of styles and colors, harness the heat energy of fireplaces and stoves and release warm moisturizing steam into the air.

Unvented or Vent-Free Appliance - an appliance that draws combustion air from inside the home. The appliance is designed to burn so efficiently that it eliminates the need for venting.

Vent-Free - gas appliance that has no need for a flue.

Zero-Clearance Fireplace - a factory-built fireplace that is constructed so that it can safely be placed close to combustible material.

Resource Guide

Central Fireplace
20502 160th St.
Greenbush, MN 56726
218-782-2575
www.centralfireplace.com
Manufacture of high quality, high performance, efficient direct-vent gas fireplaces with models that can be installed anywhere in the home, including interior walls.

Crossville Porcelain Stone/USA
PO Box 1168
Crossville, TN 38557
800-221-9093
www.crossville-ceramics.com
Founded in 1986, this is the largest domestic manufacturer of large-size porcelain stone tile and other product offerings for both residential and contract applications.

Cultured Stone® Corporation
PO Box 270
Napa, CA 94559
800-255-1727
www.culturedstone.com
A division of Owen's Corning, Cultured Stone® offers a wide variety of Cultured Stone® & Cultured Brick® products.

Design Solutions catalog:
DESA™ International
2701 Industrial Drive
Bowling Green, KY 42102
270-781-9600

www.desaint.com
Manufactures vent-free and vented hearth products, heaters, log sets, stoves, mantels, and outdoor heating products with the brand names Comfort Glow, FMI, Glow-Warm, Reddy Heater, Remington, and Vanguard.

Design Specialties
5609 West Hemlock
Milwaukee, WI 53223
414-353-4339
www.glassfireplacedoors.com
Manufacturers of fireplace accessories including in-stock and custom glass and mesh doors. Specialty trim kits and firebox surrounds are also available.

Design Specifications
1304 N. Maitland Avenue
Maitland, FL 32751
407-834-0004
The Florida design firm specializes in residential projects nationally for both new and established homes, working closely with individuals to help them achieve their own style.

DL Ackerman Design Group
El Dorado Hills, CA 95762
916-939-0252
Dee Dee Ackerman, A.M. ASID, brings her stylish touch to interior and exterior for private and commercial clients nationwide.

Empire Comfort Systems®, Inc.
918 Freeburg Avenue
Belleville, IL 62222
618-233-7420
www.empirecomfort.com
Empire Comfort Systems manufacturers a full line of gas fireplace products, residential zone heaters, commercial/industrial heating appliances, Broilmaster premium gas grills, and portable stoves and cookers.

Fire Designs
Suite 200, 310 N. Michigan Ave.
Chicago, IL 60601
312-263-5757
www.firedesigns.net
An innovative manufacturer of flame-based products that are clean burning and convenient, available for use on any deck, patio, balcony, or screened porch, or in the garden.

FireSpaces, Inc./Moberg Fireplaces
223 NW Ninth Avenue
Portland, OR 97209
503-227-0547
www.firespaces.com
For over 20 years, Walter Moberg Design, Inc. has focused on the design of fireplaces, masonry heaters, and stoves, acting as consultant to architects, builders, and manufacturers.

The Glidden Company
925 Euclid Avenue
Cleveland, OH 44115
800-GLIDDEN
www.gliddenpaint.com
In addition to paint, this leading manufacturer of architectural paints provides decorating inspiration through their Glidden Color magazine, and color visualizer CD-ROM Color @ Home.

Grand Mantel, Inc.
5552 Woodbine Ct., Suite 11
Williamsville, NY 14221
866-473-9663
www.grandmantel.com
Cabinet artisans handcraft hardwood fireplace mantels and related cabinetry. Consumers can choose from a selection of different leg and mantel styles to customize their Grand Mantel. Assembly in minutes.

Harman Stove Co./Harman Built Fireplaces
352 Mountain House Road
Halifax, PA 17032
717-362-9080
www.haarmanstoves.com
Harman's outstanding reputation was earned using the latest technology, providing outstanding efficiency, and an exceptional warranty. Their stoves and fireplaces are available throughout North America and Europe.

Hearth Classics by Yoder's
37750 Ruben Lane
Sandy, OR 97055
800-829-5470
www.hearthclassics.com
Hearth Classics incorporates the world's finest tile and stone in its hand-crafted hearth pads, fireplace surrounds and innovative mantel/surround packages. All are easily installed by homeowners or professionals.

Hearth, Patio, and Barbecue Association
1601 North Kent Street
Suite 1001
Arlington, VA 22209
703-522-0086
www.hpba.org
An international trade association that represents and promotes the interests of the hearth products industry in North America. Includes manufacturers, retailers, distributors, manufacturers' representatives, service and installation firms.

Hy-Lite Products, Inc.
101 California Avenue
Beaumont, CA 92223
1-800-827-3691
www.hy-lite.com
Acrylic blocks are about 70 percent lighter than glass blocks, and Hy-Lite can custom make windows in almost any size and shape, and guarantee against cracking, flaking, chipping, or discoloration.

Jøtul North America
400 Riverside Street
Portland, ME 04104
207-797-5912
www.jotulflame.com
Operating since 1853, this Norwegian company strives to protect the environment – creating cast iron stoves and fireplaces using recycled cast iron, manufactured with the most up-to-date machinery and hydroelectric power.

Kitchen Company
370 Sackett Point Road
North Haven, CT 06473
203-288-3866
Specializing in custom kitchens and baths, the company is situated in a 18,000-square-foot showroom and has five in-house designers to meet the design needs of their ever-growing clientele.

Lennox Hearth Products
1110 West Taft Avenue
Orange, CA 92865
800-9-LENNOX
www.lennoxhearthproducts.com
A division of Lennox International, Inc., a company known over 100 years for quality home comfort systems. Manufacturer of wood-burning and gas-fired fireplaces, fireplace inserts, stoves and chimney systems.

Majestic Fireplaces
410 Admiral Blvd.
Mississauga, Ontario Canada L5T 2N6
800-525-1898
www.majesticproducts.com
Majestic invented the first factory-built fireplace in 1954, and has been a leading producer of wood, gas, and electric fireplaces ever since.

Mantels of Yesteryear
70 West Tennessee Avenue
McCaysville, GA 30555
706-492-5534
www.mantelsofyesteryear.com
Family owned business specializing in the restoration and refinishing of antique mantels made before 1920, and the manufacture of furniture-quality reproduction mantels designed to meet modern building code demands.

Mendenhall Wood Carving
669-C Hartman Station Road
Lancaster, PA 17605
717-393-0692
Working with hand tools, artisan Duane Mendenhall carves and crafts wooden furnishings in 18th Century style, including accurate mantel reproductions.

Mendota
520 East Avenue, N.W.
Cedar Rapids, IA 52405
319-365-5267
www.mendotahearth.com
A division of Johnson Gas Appliance Company, Mendota manufactures gas fireplaces and inserts as well as gas and pellet stoves under the brand names of Allegra, Medallion, and Victoria.

Monessen Hearth Systems
149 Cleveland Drive
Paris, KY 40361 800-867-0454
www.monessenhearth.com
Manufacturing a broad line of hearth products that utilize various venting technologies in a broad choice of gas logs, gas fireplaces, and gas inserts, and a large selection of accessories.

Montigo DelRay Corporation
13120 76th Avenue
Surrey, BC V3W 2V6 Canada
800-378-3115
www.montigo.com
Manufacture a complete line of Montigo gas fireplaces, venting components, and accessories and distribute a variety of hearth products including Murustone surrounds and Seaside mantels, and cabinets.

Napoleon Fireplaces
Wolf Steel Ltd.
24 Napoleon Road RR #1
Barrie, ON L4M 4Y8 Canada
705-721-1212   www.napoleon.on.ca

Founded in 1976, this privately owned company manufactures wood and gas fireplaces, free-standing stoves, inserts, quality gas and charcoal grills, barbecue accessories, and patio heaters.

Nu-Tec Incorporated
PO Box 908
East Greenwich, RI 02818
401-738-2915
www.nutec-castings.com
Manufactures fireplaces and accessories, cookware, stoves, and outdoor decorative accessories under the brand names Amity-Bayview, Brendon, Cut-Stone, Empire Style, Georgian, Hepplewhite, Sheraton, Townsend, and Upland.

Plain & Fancy Custom Cabinetry
Route 501 & Oak Street
P.O. Box 519
Schaefferstown, PA 17088
800-447-9006
www.plainfancycabinetry.com
This 30-year-old, family-run company stands for quality workmanship at a surprisingly affordable price. Each cabinet is built using time-tested methods: mortise and tenon construction and dovetail drawers.

Sroka Design, Inc.
7307 Macarthur Blvd., Ste. 214
Bethesda, MD 20816
301-263-9100
www.srokadesign.com
This full-service residential, commercial, and hospitality interior design firm specializes in new construction and renovation projects. Their team works with architects and builders to create harmony and excellence of design.

Thermo-Rite Manufacturing Co.
PO Box 1108
Akron, OH 44309
800-321-0313   www.thermo-rite.com
The originator of tempered glass fireplace enclosures, this company is one of the hearth and fireplace accessory industry's largest suppliers of both stock and custom doors.

Toby Zack Designs, Inc.
3316 Griffin Road
Fort Lauderdale, FL 3312
954-967-8629
www.tobyzackdesigns.com
Florida Licensed Interior Designer Toby Zack has worked in both New York and Florida, creating spectacular interior designs for residential and commercial projects of both spectacular and modest scale.

Travis Industries, Inc.
10850 117th Place Northeast
Kirkland, WA 98033
425-827-9505
www.hearth.com/travis
Beginning in 1979 with the LOPI woodstove line, Travis Industries has grown to include Avalon & Fireplace Xtrordinair lines Wood, Pellet & Gas hearth heating appliances.

Tulikivi U.S., Inc.
One Penn Plaza, Ste. 3600
New York, NY 10119
800-843-3473   www.tulikivi.com
Manufacturer of efficient, healthy radiant heat fireplaces, some with bake ovens and cook tops, using solid Finnish soapstone, renown for its ability to emit warmth evenly.

Vermont Castings
410 Admiral Blvd.
Mississauga, Ontario Canada L5T 2N6
800-525-1898   www.vermontcastings.com
Founded in the hills of central Vermont in 1975, Vermont Castings is renowned as a manufacturer of premium, cast iron wood and gas stoves and gas barbecue grills.

Whalen Manufacturing Company
1270 East Murray Street
Macomb, IL 61455
800-225-1438   www.whalenco.com
Specializing in quality outdoor living products including barbecues and accessories, outdoor fireplaces, and patio and portable heaters